DASH Diet
Slow Cooker
Recipes

DASH Diet
Slow Cooker
Recipes

Easy, Delicious, and Healthy Recipes

DYLANNA**PRESS**

First edition: 2015

Disclaimer/Limit of Liability

This book is for informational purposes only. The views expressed are those of the
author alone, and should not be taken as expert, legal, or medical advice. The reader is
responsible for his or her own actions.

Every attempt has been made to verify the accuracy of the information in this
publication. However, neither the author nor the publisher assumes any responsibility
for errors, omissions, or contrary interpretation of the material contained herein.

This book is not intended to provide medical advice. Please see your health care
professional before embarking on any new diet or exercise program. The reader should
regularly consult a physician in matters relating to his/her health and particularly with
respect to any symptoms that may require diagnosis or medical attention.

Photo credits: Canstock Photo

Contents

Introduction

The DASH diet has once again been named the healthiest diet by top nutrition experts and there's no better time to start reaping the rewards of this smart, sensible eating plan. Eating the DASH diet way does not have to be boring, in fact, it contains the most delicious foods around – lean meats, whole grains, lots of fresh fruits and vegetables, and flavorful herbs and spices. So whether you are just starting out on the DASH diet or have been eating low-sodium for years, the *DASH Diet Slow Cooker Recipes: Easy, Delicious, and Healthy Recipes* is going to help you make delicious, healthy meals without spending a lot of time in the kitchen.

For this book, we've collected the best slow cooker recipes and adapted them to the DASH diet to create mouthwatering, family-pleasing dishes that can all be prepared easily and then cooked in your slow cooker while you're off doing other things. There's really nothing better than coming home at the end of a hectic day to the smell of tonight's dinner already prepared and waiting to be eaten.

These recipes feature fresh, whole foods and include a wide variety of recipes to appeal to every taste from classic dishes to new twists that just may become your new favorites. In addition, each recipe has less than 500 mg of sodium per serving, many a lot less than that.

In addition to recipes, the book includes a brief overview of the DASH diet as well as tips on how to get the most out of your slow cooker.

Thanks for reading and happy cooking!

About the DASH Diet

The DASH diet is one of the most researched and well-respected diets available today. It is not a fad diet or a quick weight-loss scheme, but instead a guide to a healthier way of eating and living.

The DASH diet was developed to lower blood pressure, one of the leading factors in heart disease. In addition to lowering blood pressure, the diet has been found to be more nutritious and lead to better health in all areas when compared with the standard American diet (SAD).

DASH stands for Dietary Approaches to Stop Hypertension and it is designed as a life-long approach to treating or preventing hypertension (high blood pressure). It is often prescribed by doctors as a first step in dealing with pre-hypertension as a way of avoiding blood pressure medications.

The DASH diet focuses on reducing the amount of sodium in your diet and increasing nutrient-rich foods such as fruits, vegetables, and whole grains. Research has shown that by following the DASH diet you can reduce your blood pressure by as much as 12 points, which is as effective as taking a medication.[1]

In addition to helping to lower blood pressure, the DASH diet has many other health benefits. These include:

- decreased risk of heart disease
- decreased risk of cancer
- decreased risk of diabetes
- decreased risk of stroke
- lower cholesterol levels
- helps to prevent osteoporosis
- helps to promote weight loss

---

[1] http://www.health.harvard.edu/press_releases/diet-can-lower-blood-pressure-as-much-as-taking-a-medication

For these reasons, the DASH diet is a smart choice for anyone looking to improve their health.

Daily Nutrient Goals for the DASH Diet

Below are the daily nutrient guidelines set by the National Heart, Lung, and Blood Institute:[2]

Daily Nutrient Goals for the DASH Diet

Total fat: 27% of calories
Saturated fat: 6% of calories
Protein: 18% of calories
Carbohydrate: 55% of calories
Cholesterol: 150 mg
Sodium: 2,300 mg/1,500 mg*
Potassium: 4,700 mg
Calcium: 1,250 mg
Magnesium: 500 mg
Fiber: 30 g

* 1,500 mg sodium has been found to be even better for lowering blood pressure. It was particularly effective for middle-aged and older individuals, African Americans, and those who already had high blood pressure. g = grams; mg = milligrams

---

It is recommended that you consult with your doctor to determine whether you should follow the 2,300 or 1,500 mg sodium recommendations.

---

[2] http://www.nhlbi.nih.gov/health/resources/heart/hbp-dash-how-plan-html

DASH Diet Eating Plan

The DASH diet eating plan focuses on including fresh fruits and vegetables, low-fat dairy products, and lean sources of protein into your daily diet. It aims to reduce the amount of salt and sodium, added sugar, fats, and red meat. The diet is rich in nutrients that promote low blood pressure including potassium, magnesium, calcium, protein, and fiber.

Below are the recommendations for daily servings based on a 2,000 calorie per day diet. These guidelines were developed by the National Institutes of Health.

Whole grains: 6 to 8 servings per day

This category includes breads, pasta, oats, cereals, rice, quinoa, rye as well as other grains. It is recommended that you choose whole grains over white and refined grains.

Sample servings:

- 1 slice bread
- 1 ounce cereal
- ½ cup cooked pasta or rice

Vegetables: 4 to 6 servings per day

This category includes asparagus, broccoli, Brussels sprouts, carrots, celery, green beans, green leafy vegetables, kale, lettuce, peppers, potatoes, pumpkin, spinach, squash, sweet potatoes, tomatoes, and turnips as well as other vegetables.

Sample servings:

- 1 cup leafy greens
- ½ cup cooked or raw vegetables
- ½ cup vegetable juice

Fruits: 4 to 6 servings per day

This category includes apples, bananas, cherries, dates, grapes, grapefruit, lemons, mangoes, melons, peaches, pears, pineapple, raisins, strawberries, and watermelon as well as other fruits.

Sample servings:

- 1 medium apple, peach, or pear
- ½ cup fresh, frozen, or canned fruit
- ¼ dried fruit

Dairy products: 2 to 3 servings per day

This category includes low-fat/nonfat milk, buttermilk, low-fat/nonfat cheeses, and low-fat/nonfat yogurt.

Sample servings:

- 1 cup (8 ounces) milk or yogurt
- 1 ½ ounces cheese

Lean protein: 3 to 6 servings per day

This category includes meats, poultry, fish, and eggs. Choose lean cuts of meat and trim away excess fat. Remove skin from poultry.

Sample servings:

- 1 egg
- 1 ounce cooked meat (to visualize, 4 ounces is about the size of a deck of cards)

Nuts, seeds, legumes: 3 to 5 servings per week

This category includes almonds, black beans, hazelnuts, kidney beans, legumes, lentils, peanuts, pumpkin seeds, split peas, and sunflower seeds as well other nuts, seeds, and legumes.

Sample servings:

- 1/3 cup (1 ½ ounces) nuts

- 2 tablespoons peanut butter
- 2 tablespoons sunflower seeds
- ½ cup cooked legumes

Fats and oils: 2-3 serving per day

This category includes coconut oil, ghee, low-fat mayonnaise, margarine, olive oil, salad dressings, and vegetable oils.

Sample servings:

- 1 teaspoon olive oil
- 1 teaspoon margarine
- 1 tablespoons mayonnaise
- 2 tablespoons salad dressing

Sweets and sugars: 5 or less per week

This category includes fruit-flavored gelatin, candy, jelly, maple syrup, sorbet, and sugar

Sample servings:

- 1 tablespoon sugar
- 1 tablespoon jam
- ½ cup sorbet

The table below outlines the number of recommended daily servings for various calorie levels. The amount of calories needed per day depends on a number of factors including your current age, weight, gender, and activity level.

DASH Eating Plan—Number of Daily Servings for Other Calorie Levels

	Servings/Day		
Food Groups	1,600 calories/day	2,600 calories/day	3,100 calories/day
Grains	6	10-11	12-13
Vegetables	3-4	5-6	6
Fruits	4	5-6	6
Nonfat or lowfat dairy products	2-3	3	3-4
Lean meats, poultry, and fish	3-6	6	6-9
Nuts, seeds, and legumes	3/week	1	1
Fats and oils	2	3	4
Sweets and sugars	0	less than 2	less than 2

Spices and Seasonings

If you are used to seasoning your food with salt, then doing without may take some getting used to it. But rest assured that there are many alternative ways to amp up the flavor of your food without resorting to shaking salt on it. As an added benefit, many herbs and spices contain powerful antioxidants and other properties that are highly beneficial to your health. Below is a list of herbs and spices that can be used to replace salt on the DASH diet to add flavor to your food.

Basil: Basil is one of the most common herbs used in cooking. It has a slightly sweet and pungent taste.

Bay leaves: These sweet and aromatic leaves are often used to enhance the flavor of meats, stews, and other dishes.

Cardamom: Cardamom is a popular spice in Indian cooking with a peppery and citrusy taste.

Cayenne: Cayenne has a hot and peppery flavor that will definitely spice up a dish. Also called red chili pepper.

Cinnamon: Cinnamon can help to regulate blood sugar and lower cholesterol.

Garlic/garlic powder: Garlic, whether fresh or in powder form, is a great alternative to salt as it not only enhances taste but has many known health-boosting properties.

Ginger: Ginger can be used either fresh or as a powder and in addition to adding flavor has many health benefits.

Lemon juice: A squeeze of lemon juice adds a fresh citrusy flavor that can enhance the flavor of many foods.

Onion powder: Onion powder has a strong taste that many people love, but use sparingly or its flavor can overpower a dish.

Pepper (black): You may think of salt and pepper as a dynamic duo but pepper is perfectly capable of standing alone. It will enhance the flavor of any dish. Choose freshly ground black pepper for a more distinct and intense taste.

Top Hidden Sources of Sodium

You may think that just passing on the salt shaker will be enough to lower the amount of sodium in your diet. However, you might be surprised to learn about the many products that contain hidden sodium. Here are some of the top culprits.

Sodium in Common Foods

Bread and baked goods: Bread is one of the top sources of dietary sodium. One slice of bread can contain anywhere from 350-700 milligrams of sodium. Read labels carefully and choose a brand with the lowest sodium content. Other baked goods such as doughnuts, muffins, and cakes made from baking mixes are also loaded with sodium.

Breakfast cereals: The amount of salt in cereals varies widely so it is important to read labels carefully.

Condiments and sauces: The majority of store-bought condiments such as ketchup, mustard, salad dressings, soy sauce, relish, barbecue sauce, and jarred spaghetti sauce are loaded with sodium. Read labels carefully and buy reduced or no-sodium products whenever possible. Even better, make your own homemade sauces and dressings.

Cheese and dairy products: Most people don't think of salt when it comes to cheese, but salt is used in the cheese-making process and they are a significant source of sodium in the diet. Milk also contains sodium, 120 milligrams per half-cup serving.

Canned foods: Salt is used to flavor and preserve most canned foods such as soups, stews, and vegetables. A can of Campbell's chicken noodle soup has a whopping 900 milligrams of sodium per serving. Canned beans are also high in sodium content. Look for low-salt and salt-free versions or make your own.

Stocking Your Kitchen

A big part of preparing meals without a lot of fuss is having the ingredients you need on hand. Keeping your pantry stocked with a few essentials will go a long way toward making it easy to prepare a quick and healthy DASH diet meal.

Cleaning Out

If you're committed to incorporating the DASH diet principles into your eating, the first thing you need to do is clean out your refrigerator, freezer, and pantry. Look carefully at all of the labels of everything in your kitchen. Get rid of anything that is high in sodium, sugar, white flour, or saturated and trans fats.

Restocking

Now that you've gotten rid of all the foods that may be causing problems, it's time to stock up on a few basics to keep on hand.

Pantry Items

- 100% whole-wheat bread (small slice) and pita pockets
- Applesauce, unsweetened
- Baking powder and baking soda
- Beans (dried and/or canned)
- Brown rice
- Brown sugar
- Chicken, beef and/or vegetable broth, low-sodium
- Cornstarch or arrowroot
- Dried fruit and nuts
- Flour (unbleached and whole wheat)
- Granola bars, low-fat

- Marinade, low-sodium – try the Mrs. Dash brand
- Oatmeal (whole oats or quick cooking, not instant)
- Olive and canola oils
- Pretzels (unsalted)
- Quinoa
- Reduced-sodium ketchup, deli mustard, "lite" mayonnaise
- Salad dressings, low-sodium, a good brand to try is Consorzio
- Salsa
- Tomato sauce, low-sodium
- Tomatoes, canned, no-salt-added
- Tuna packed in water
- Vegetable oil spray
- Vinegar (balsamic and white wine)
- Whole-grain cereals (shredded wheat, toasted oat, bran flakes)
- Whole-wheat pasta
- Whole-wheat snack crackers, low-sodium

Refrigerator Items

- Bottled lemon juice
- Eggs and/or egg substitute
- Fresh fruit
- Fresh vegetables
- Fresh-pack salad greens
- Garlic
- Lemons
- Lime
- Low-fat and nonfat yogurt
- Low-fat cottage cheese
- Low-fat or nonfat milk
- Natural peanut butter
- Onions
- Reduced-fat string cheese
- Reduced-fat, low-sodium deli meat
- Reduced-sodium soy sauce and teriyaki sauce

- Tortillas, whole wheat or corn
- Trans-fat-free margarine

Freezer Items

- Fish
- Frozen fruit (without added sugar)
- Frozen vegetables (no sauces or salt)
- Homemade soups and broth – freeze in single servings
- Lean meats
- Low-calorie frozen desserts

Slow Cooker Essentials

Slow cookers are the greatest invention of all time. Okay, that might be a slight exaggeration, but there really is no better way to prepare delicious, flavorful meals with so little effort.

In addition, with a slow cooker, you can save money by buying cheaper cuts of meat because when cooked over 6-8 hours they will become tender and release their rich flavors.

Choosing a Slow Cooker

There are many styles and sizes of slow cookers available today. They range in size from very small, which hold 1 1/2 to 2 quarts, to large, which hold up to 7 quarts. The most versatile and common size for a slow cooker is a 6-quart model and that is the size used for the recipes in this book. However, they can be adapted to a smaller or larger cooker size.

They come in variety of shapes as well—round, oval, even rectangular. An oval shape is recommended over a round one, because they tend to have less hot spots.

Some slow cooker models feature a stovetop safe insert, and if you are in the market for a new slow cooker then it is highly recommended that you choose this option. Many recipes require that you sauté or brown the meats and vegetables before adding them to the slow cooker and with these models there is no need to dirty another pan.

Another feature to look for is programmability. While manual slow cookers are cheaper, the ability to automatically switch to warm after a certain period of time can be a big plus if you work long days and don't want to come home and find an overcooked meal waiting for you.

Tips for Using Your Slow Cooker

Do not overfill your slow cooker. Only fill about two-thirds full.

Do not add frozen ingredients directly to slow cooker. This can cause food to spend too much time in the food safety "danger zone" and potentially increase the chances of food-borne illnesses. Always thaw ingredients before adding to slow cooker.

Cook meat and poultry to the FDA minimum internal temperature recommendations (see table). Use an instant-read thermometer to test doneness.

Do not lift cover while cooking more than absolutely necessary. Doing so will cause the temperature to drop to potentially unsafe levels.

Never reheat foods using the slow cooker.

Brown meats before adding to slow cooker. Although it is nice to just throw all the ingredients in the slow cooker and let it cook, the majority of recipes will be enhanced by first browning the meats on the stovetop. Taking this extra step will lead to more flavorful dishes.

Sautéing onions and garlic in oil for a couple of minutes before adding them to the slow cooker will likewise increase the richness and flavor of the dish.

Choose the right cut of meat. Many people believe that the leanest cuts of meat are the best. However, when cooking in the slow cooker the opposite is true. When lean meats are cooked for a long time they can end up dry and tough. This is why slow cookers are ideal for more inexpensive, tougher, and fattier cuts of meat. The slow cooking breaks them down and leaves a tender, juicy piece of meat.

Don't add too much liquid. Since you are cooking with the lid on, very little liquid will evaporate during cooking. If too much liquid is added, you will have a thin, watery sauce.

Use a liner for easy clean up. Lining your slow cooker will make for incredibly easy clean up.

Minimum Internal Temperature for Doneness

The USDA recommends the following minimum internal temperatures for meats and poultry. To accurately measure temperature, stick and instant-read thermometer into the center of the meat, being careful to not let the thermometer touch the bone.

Type of Meat (degrees F)	Minimum Internal Temperature
Beef	145
Pork	145
Lamb	145
Veal	145
Ground meat	160
Poultry	165

Part II

Recipes

Breakfast Dishes

Apple-Cinnamon Baked Oatmeal

This oatmeal recipe is cooked in the slow cooker so you can wake up to a warm and satisfying breakfast without any fuss.

Servings: 8

Ingredients:

- **2 cups steel cut oats**
- **8 cups water**
- **1 tsp cinnamon**
- **1/2 tsp allspice**
- **1/2 tsp nutmeg**
- **1/4 cup brown sugar**
- **1 tsp vanilla extract**
- **2 apples, diced**
- **1 cup raisins**
- **1/2 cup unsalted, roasted walnuts, chopped**

Directions:

1. Spray slow cooker with nonstick cooking spray.
2. Add all ingredients to slow cooker except for walnuts. Mix well to combine.
3. Set slow cooker to low setting and cook for 8 hours.
4. Serve topped with chopped walnuts

Nutritional Information (per serving)
Calories: 312
Sodium: 4 mg
Protein: 9 g
Carbs: 60 g
Fat: 7.5 g
Sugar: 23 g

Note: Be sure to use steel cut oats for this recipe (not instant or rolled oats) or you may end up with a sticky mess.

Banana-Nut Oatmeal

Another flavorful version of oatmeal that will be ready for you when you wake up in the morning.

Servings: 4

Ingredients:

- 1 cup steel cut oats
- 1 banana, mashed
- 1/3 cup walnuts, chopped
- 2 cups skim milk
- 2 cups water
- 1/3 cup honey
- 2 teaspoons cinnamon
- 1/2 teaspoon nutmeg
- 1 teaspoon vanilla extract
- 1/2 teaspoon salt

Directions:

1. Place all ingredients in slow cooker. Stir well, cover, and cook on low for 8 hours.
2. Serve with extra banana slices and walnuts on top.

Nutritional Information (per serving)
Calories: 310
Sodium: 365 mg
Protein: 11 g
Carbs: 42 g
Dietary Fiber: 6 g
Fat: 9 g

Homemade Greek-Style Yogurt

If you eat a lot of yogurt (and you should!) then you know it can get expensive. Making your own is really simple with the help of your slow cooker.

Servings: 8 (1 cup size)
Ingredients:
- **1/2 gallon 2 percent milk**
- **1 cup powdered milk (this is optional but does make the yogurt thicker)**
- **½ cup live yogurt culture (can use regular plain yogurt)**
- **Thermometer**
- **Small blanket**
- **Cheesecloth for straining**

Directions:
1. Pour milk into slow cooker. Stir in powdered milk. Heat the milk in the slow cooker on high until it reaches 180 degrees F (about 1-2 hours depending on your cooker). Turn off slow cooker and let milk cool to 110 degrees F. Stir in live yogurt culture and mix until completely blended. Wrap the slow cooker (which is turned off) in a blanket to keep the heat in. Let sit for 6-8 hours.
2. Take lid of slow cooker. To make thick, Greek-style yogurt you will need to drain the whey (the liquid on top of the yogurt) out of the yogurt. To do this, place a few layers of cheesecloth in a colander. Place the colander over a large bowl. Add the yogurt to the colander and let it drain in the refrigerator for a couple of hours until it has reached the consistency you like. You now have delicious Greek yogurt!
3. Pour the yogurt into mason jars (or other containers) and store in the refrigerator for 7-10 days.

Nutritional Information (per serving)

Calories: 143	Total Carbs: 19 g
Total Fat: 3.5 g	Dietary Fiber: 0 g
Sodium: 159 mg	Protein: 18 g

Breakfast Casserole

Perfect for a relaxing Sunday brunch.

Servings: 8

Ingredients:

- **4 cups frozen hash browns**
- **12 eggs**
- **1/2 cup lowfat milk**
- **10 ounces sausage, cooked, low-sodium**
- **8 ounces cheddar cheese, shredded**
- **2 garlic cloves, minced**
- **1 medium onion, diced**
- **1/2 red bell pepper, diced**
- **Freshly ground black pepper**

Directions:

1. Spray bottom of slow cooker with cooking spray.
2. Crack eggs into large bowl. Add milk, mustard, and black pepper and whisk until combined.
3. Spread 1/2 hash browns on bottom of slow cooker. Top with 1/2 each: sausage, cheese, garlic, onion, bell pepper. Add second layer of hash browns, sausage, cheese, garlic, onion, and bell pepper.
4. Pour egg mixture over layers. Cover, and cook on low setting for 4 to 5 hours or on high for 2 to 3 hours, until eggs are set.

Nutritional Information (per serving)
Calories: 336
Total Fat: 23 g
Sodium: 468 mg
Total Carbs: 13 g
Protein: 19 g

Soups

Chicken Broth

*The slow cooker is perfect for making your own chicken broth. It is
perfect for using as a base in your soups and other recipes.*

Servings: 5

Ingredients:

- **2 pounds bone-in chicken pieces (any type will do)**
- **6 cups water**
- **2 celery stalks, chopped**
- **2 medium carrots, chopped**
- **1 medium onion, chopped**
- **1 tablespoon basil, dried**

Directions:

1. Place all ingredients into slow cooker.
2. Cover and cook on low for 8 to 10 hours. Strain before using.
   Discard vegetables. Chicken can be used in soup or other recipe.

Nutritional information (per serving)
Calories: 247
Total Fat: 15 g
Sodium: 99 mg
Total Carbs: 6 g
Dietary Fiber: 1.8 g
Protein: 22 g

Potato Leek Soup with Beans

This soup is hearty enough to make a main dish.

Servings: 8

Ingredients:

- **2 leeks**
- **1/2 of a medium white onion**
- **2 tablespoons unsalted butter**
- **4 medium potatoes, peeled and cubed**
- **1/2 parsnip, diced**
- **4 cups vegetable broth, low-sodium (homemade or store bought)**
- **2 sprigs fresh rosemary**
- **2 sprigs fresh thyme**
- **1 can nonfat evaporated milk**
- **1 can white beans (cannellini or any other white bean), no-salt-added, drained and rinsed**
- **Freshly ground black pepper, to taste**

Directions:

1. Slice the dark green tops off the leeks and the bottom roots off. You will be using only the white and light green parts of the leek, about 4-6 inches of leek. Rinse the leeks, then chop up into small slices. Dice the white onion. In a skillet, melt the unsalted butter over medium heat. Sauté the leek and onion for about 5 minutes, or until they begin to soften. Remove from heat and pour the leek, onion, and any melted butter still there into the slow cooker.
2. Add the potatoes, parsnip, broth, rosemary, thyme, evaporated milk, and white beans into the slow cooker. Stir well.

3. Cover and cook on low for 6-7 hours or high for 4-5 until potatoes and parsnip are soft.
4. Use and immersion blender to puree soup to desired consistency. Alternatively, transfer the contents to a blender or large food processor, and puree it. (This may take two batches if your blender or processor is small.) Return the puree to the slow cooker and heat through - about 15 minutes. Season with pepper to taste. Serve hot.

Nutritional Information (per serving)

Calories: 251.9

Total Fat: 3.4 g

Sodium: 109.2 mg

Total Carbs: 44.1 g

Dietary Fiber: 6.4 g

Protein: 11.2 g

Crockpot French Onion Soup

Servings: 8-10

Ingredients:

- **4 medium sweet onions, thinly sliced**
- **3 garlic cloves, minced**
- **4 tablespoons of butter, unsalted**
- **2 tablespoons brown sugar**
- **2 tablespoons balsamic vinegar**
- **3 tablespoons all-purpose flour**
- **8 ounces of beer**
- **64 ounces of low-sodium beef stock**
- **2 tablespoons fresh thyme**
- **1/2 teaspoon black pepper**
- **French bread**
- **8-10 pieces Gruyere cheese, sliced**

Directions:

1. Heat a medium size skillet over medium heat. Add onions, garlic, and butter, and sauté until onions soften, about 3-4 minutes. Add brown sugar and vinegar and mix until combined. Add to slow cooker.
2. Add in flour, beer, beef stock, thyme, and pepper. Stir, cover, and cook on low setting for 6-8 hours.
3. Before serving, cut French bread into slices about an inch-thick. Fill oven-safe soup bowls with soup, top with slice of bread and a slice of cheese. Set under the broiler for 2-3 minutes, or until cheese is bubbly and golden brown. Serve at once.

Nutritional information (per serving)
Calories: 140
Total Fat: 4.5 g

Sodium: 505 mg
Total Carbs: 19 g
Dietary Fiber: 2 g
Protein: 5 g

Slow Cooker Chicken Noodle Soup

Nothing is more soothing than home-cooked chicken noodle soup.

Servings: 8

Ingredients:

- **2 pounds chicken, skinless and boneless, cut into 2" pieces**
- **6 cups low-sodium chicken broth**
- **1/2 teaspoon crushed red pepper flakes**
- **1 cup celery, diced**
- **4 carrots, sliced**
- **1 small onion, diced**
- **3 cloves garlic, minced**
- **1/4 cup fresh, chopped, Italian parsley**
- **1/2 teaspoon black pepper**
- **Pinch sea salt**
- **8 ounces whole wheat noodles**

Directions:

1. Add all ingredients, except the noodles, in the slow cooker and cook for 6-8 hours on low, or until carrots are tender.
2. The last hour of cooking time, add in the noodles and continue cooking one additional hour or until pasta is to desired doneness.

Nutritional information (per serving)
Calories: 149
Total Fat: 2 g
Sodium: 150 mg
Total Carbs: 14 g
Dietary Fiber: 2 g
Protein: 11 g

Hearty Minestrone Soup

This soup provides a nice vegetarian dinner. Serve with some crusty whole-grain bread.

Servings: 8

Ingredients:

- **4 cups tomato juice, low-sodium**
- **4 cups vegetable broth, low-sodium**
- **1 medium onion, chopped**
- **4 cloves garlic, diced**
- **3 stalks celery, diced**
- **3 large carrots, sliced**
- **2 medium zucchini, chopped**
- **1 red pepper, diced**
- **1 (15 ounce) can white beans, rinsed and drained**
- **1 cup dried Stelline pasta (can substitute orzo, farfalline, or other small pasta)**
- **2 teaspoons dried basil**
- **2 teaspoons dried oregano**
- **Freshly ground black pepper, to taste**

Directions:

1. Place all ingredients into slow cooker. Cover, and cook on low for 8-9 hours or high for 4-5 hours, until vegetables are tender.

Nutritional information (per serving)
Calories: 204
Total Fat: 1 g
Sodium: 180 mg
Total Carbs: 40 g
Protein: 9 g

New England Clam Chowder

This hearty chowder is rich with potatoes and clams.

Servings: 10

Ingredients:

- **2 cups skim milk**
- **2 cups 1% milk**
- **2 tablespoons butter, unsalted**
- **3 medium potatoes, peeled and diced**
- **1 medium yellow onion, chopped**
- **2 celery stalks, chopped**
- **1 bag of frozen sweet corn**
- **16 ounces of fresh clams in juice**

Directions:

1   Place all ingredients into slow cooker.
2   Cover and cook 2-3 hours on high setting or 4-6 hours on low setting. Onions should be soft and potato should be tender.

Nutritional Information (per serving)
Calories: 225.8
Total Fat: 3.8 g
Sodium: 112.7 mg
Total Carbs: 34.1 g
Dietary Fiber: 2.4 g
Protein: 5 g

Crock-Pot Lobster Bisque

Servings: 6-8

Ingredients:

- 1 teaspoon olive oil
- 2 shallots, minced
- 1 clove garlic, minced
- 2 (14.5 ounce) cans diced tomatoes, no salt added
- 1 (32 ounce) carton low-sodium chicken broth (or homemade)
- 1 tablespoon Old Bay seasoning
- 1 teaspoon dried dill
- 1/4 cup fresh parsley, chopped
- 1 teaspoon freshly ground black pepper
- 1/2 teaspoon paprika
- 3 lobster tails
- 1 pint heavy cream

Directions:

1. Heat olive oil in skillet over medium heat. Add shallots and garlic and sauté for 2-3 minutes. Add shallot and garlic mixture to slow cooker.
2. Add tomatoes, chicken broth, Old Bay seasoning, dill, parsley, pepper, and paprika to slow cooker.
3. Using a sharp knife cut off the fan part of the end of the lobsters and add those to slow cooker, reserving the lobster tails for later.
4. Stir, cover, and cook on low setting for 6 hours or high setting for 3 hours.
5. Remove the lobster tail ends from cooker and discard.

6. Using an immersion blender puree the soup mixture to your desired chunkiness. Can also use a regular blender, working in batches.
7. Add lobster tails to the soup, cover, and cook about an hour on low or until the shells turn red and the lobster meat is cooked.
8. Remove lobster tails from the soup and let cool slightly. Cut each lobster tail in half long-ways and remove the lobster flesh from the shells. Discard shells and roughly chop lobster meat and add back into the soup.
9. Add the cream and stir.

Nutritional information (per serving)
Calories: 380
Total Fat: 27 g
Sodium: 330 mg
Total Carbs: 15 g
Dietary Fiber: 1 g
Protein: 22 g

Meatball Soup

This hearty soup is perfect on a cold winter day.

Servings: 6

Ingredients:

For the meatballs:

- 1 pound ground beef, lean (90/10)
- ½ pound ground pork
- 1/4 cup bread crumbs
- 3 garlic cloves, minced
- 1 small yellow onion, finely chopped
- 1 egg, beaten
- 1 tablespoon Italian seasoning
- 1 teaspoon black pepper
- 2 tablespoons olive oil

For the soup:

- 4 slices bacon, cut into pieces
- 3 cloves garlic, minced
- 1 medium zucchini, chopped
- 1 medium yellow squash, chopped
- 2 carrots, sliced thin
- 1 small onion, diced fine
- 1 teaspoon oregano
- 1 teaspoon marjoram
- 1 teaspoon garlic powder
- 4 cups chicken broth, low sodium
- 1 can (14.5 ounces) diced tomatoes, no salt added

Directions:

1. In a large bowl, mix together all ingredients for meatballs except for olive oil. Form into balls about 1 ½ to 2 inches in diameter.
2. Heat olive oil in large skillet over medium heat. Add meatballs and cook until all sides are browned. Remove meatballs and set aside. Add bacon to pan and sauté for 4-5 minutes. Add garlic and sauté for another 2 minutes.
3. Place bacon and garlic (along with drippings) into slow cooker. Place meatballs on top.
4. Add in all remaining ingredients. Stir gently to mix.
5. Cover and cook on low setting for 8 hours or on high setting for 5 hours.

Nutritional Information (per serving)
Calories: 295
Total Fat: 17 g
Sodium: 195 mg
Total Carbs: 11 g
Protein: 21 g

Chicken Tortilla Soup

This is a healthier, low-sodium version of a popular soup.

Servings: 8

Ingredients:

- 1 pound chicken, boneless and skinless, cut into bite-size pieces
- 1 (15 ounce) can whole tomatoes, mashed
- 1 (10 ounce) can enchilada sauce
- 1 medium onion, chopped
- 2 chili peppers, chopped
- 3 cloves garlic, minced
- 2 cups water
- 2 cups low-sodium chicken broth
- 1 (10 ounce) package frozen corn
- 2 teaspoons cumin
- 2 teaspoons chili powder
- 1/2 teaspoon salt
- 1/2 teaspoon freshly ground black pepper
- 1 bay leaf
- 1 tablespoon fresh cilantro, chopped
- 8 corn tortillas

Directions:

1. Place chicken, tomatoes, enchilada sauce, onion, pepper, and garlic into slow cooker. Add in water, chicken broth and corn. Season with cumin, chili powder, salt, pepper, bay leaf, and cilantro.
2. Cover and cook on low for 7-8 hours or high for 3-4 hours.

3   Cut tortillas into strips. Place on baking sheet and cook in preheated 400 degree F oven for about 10 minutes until crisp.
4   Serve soup with tortilla strips sprinkled on top.

Note: May also be topped with fresh avocado slices, shredded cheese, or fresh cilantro.

Nutritional information (per serving)
Calories: 210
Total Fat: 6.8 g
Sodium: 398 mg
Total Carbs: 24 g
Dietary Fiber: 3.9 g
Protein: 15 g

Corn and Shrimp Chowder

Most recipes for corn and shrimp chowder have too much sodium for the DASH diet. Here we have reduced the sodium without reducing the flavor.

Servings: 6
Ingredients:

- **3 cups chicken broth, low-sodium**
- **2 cups water**
- **2 (16 ounce) bags frozen corn**
- **1 medium yellow onion, chopped**
- **2 large carrots, chopped**
- **1 red bell pepper, chopped**
- **3 medium potatoes, diced**
- **2 bay leaves**
- **2 teaspoons Old Bay seasoning**
- **1 teaspoon cayenne pepper**
- **1 pound medium shrimp, peeled and deveined**
- **1/2 cup whole milk**
- **1/3 cup fresh parsley**
- **Freshly ground black pepper, to taste**

Directions:

1. Add chicken broth, water, corn, onion, carrots, pepper, potatoes, bay leaves, Old Bay, and cayenne pepper to slow cooker. Cover and cook on low for 5-6 hours, until vegetables are tender.
2. Using an immersion blender, puree soup until desired consistency is reached. Alternatively, working in batches, blend soup in traditional blender until desired consistency is reached and return to slow cooker.
3. Add shrimp and milk, stir, cover, and cook for another 15 minutes until shrimp are pink.
4. Remove bay leaves, sprinkle with parsley, and season with black pepper before serving.

Nutritional information (per serving)

Calories: 550	Total Carbs: 97 g
Total Fat: 6 g	Dietary Fiber: 6 g
Sodium: 391 mg	Protein: 31 g

Split Pea Soup

This classic soup works well in the slow cooker.

Servings: 6

Ingredients:

- **7 cups chicken broth, low-sodium**
- **1 bag green or yellow split peas, rinsed and drained**
- **1 medium onion, diced**
- **4 carrots, diced**
- **1 celery stalk, diced**
- **1/2 red bell pepper, diced**
- **3 cloves garlic, minced**
- **1 teaspoon dried thyme**
- **1 bay leaf**
- **1 ham hock**
- **Freshly ground black pepper, to taste**

Directions:

1. Add all ingredients to slow cooker. Stir, cover, and cook on high for 6-7 hours or until split peas are creamy.
2. Remove ham hocks. Remove and discard skin and bones. Dice meat and return to slow cooker. Remove bay leaf before serving.

Nutritional Information (per serving)
Calories: 370
Sodium: 180 mg
Protein: 28 g
Carbs: 62 g
Dietary Fiber: 25 g
Fat: 3.5 g

Poultry Dishes

Mexican Chicken Stew

This spicy stew is very easy to prepare.

Servings: 12

Ingredients:

- **4 chicken breasts, boneless and skinless**
- **1 (15.5 ounce) can whole kernel corn, no-salt added**
- **1 (15.5 ounce) can kidney beans, no-sodium added**
- **1 (15.5 ounce) can black beans, no-sodium added**
- **1 (15.5 ounce) can diced tomatoes, no-salt added**
- **1 medium yellow onion, diced**
- **1 green bell pepper, diced**
- **1 (15.5 ounce) can tomato sauce, no-salt added**
- **2 tablespoons chili powder**
- **2 teaspoons onion powder**
- **2 teaspoons ground cumin**
- **1 teaspoon garlic powder**
- **1 teaspoon paprika**
- **1 teaspoon ground oregano**

Directions:

1. Place chicken breasts in slow cooker. Add remaining ingredients, and stir gently, leaving chicken on bottom.
2. Cover and cook on high for 3-4 hours or low for 5-6 hours. Remove chicken breasts and shred or chop them and add back to stew. Mix well before serving.

Nutritional Information (per serving)
Calories: 208.5
Total Fat: 1.6 g
Sodium: 162.3 mg
Carbs: 23.3 g
Dietary Fiber: 5.9 g
Protein: 25.6 g

Crockpot Chicken Fajitas

Servings: 4

Ingredients:

- **1 pound chicken breast, boneless and skinless**
- **1 medium onion, sliced into strips**
- **1 medium red bell pepper, sliced into strips**
- **1 medium green bell pepper, sliced into strips**
- **3 garlic cloves, minced**
- **1 tablespoon taco seasoning**
- **1 cup salsa**

Directions:

1 Place chicken breast in crockpot. Cut onion, peppers, and garlic and place on top of chicken. Top with salsa. Cover and cook for 7-8 hours on low setting or 5-6 hours on high.
2 Shred chicken and serve with tortillas.

Nutritional Info (per serving)
Calories: 176.0
Total Fat: 1.6 g
Sodium: 156.2 mg
Total Carbs: 11.3 g
Dietary Fiber: 1.6 g
Protein: 27.2 g

Black Bean Chicken

This is a very simple recipe but it is very tasty.

Servings: 6

Ingredients:

- **1 pound boneless, skinless chicken breasts**
- **2 15-ounce cans black beans, low-sodium, rinsed and drained**
- **2 cups salsa (if buying jarred, make sure it is low sodium)**
- **1/2 cup brown rice (uncooked)**

Directions:

- Place chicken breasts in slow cooker.
- Pour beans, rice, and salsa over chicken. Stir to combine.
- Cover and cook on low for 8-10 hours. Serve hot.

Nutritional Information (per serving)
Calories: 307.3
Total Fat: 2.9 g
Sodium: 146.4 mg
Total Carbs: 40.0 g
Dietary Fiber: 13.0 g
Protein: 30 g

Turkey Chili

Servings: 8

Ingredients:

- **1 tablespoon olive oil**
- **1 pound ground turkey**
- **2 (10.75 ounce) cans tomato soup, low-sodium**
- **2 (15 ounce) cans red kidney beans, low-sodium, rinsed and drained**
- **1 (15 ounce) can black beans, drained**
- **1/2 medium onion, chopped**
- **2 tablespoons chili powder**
- **1 teaspoon red pepper flakes**
- **1/2 tablespoon garlic powder**
- **1/2 tablespoon ground cumin**
- **Freshly ground black pepper, to taste**
- **½ teaspoon ground allspice**

Directions:

1. Heat the oil in a skillet over medium heat. Add ground turkey to skillet, and cook until browned, drain.
2. Spray slow cooker with cooking spray, and add turkey, tomato soup, kidney beans, black beans, and onion. Season with chili powder, red pepper flakes, garlic powder, cumin, black pepper, allspice, and salt.
3. Cover and cook 7-8 hours on low setting or 4-5 hours on high setting.

Nutritional information (per serving)
Calories: 520
Total Fat: 8 g
Sodium: 390 mg
Total Carbs: 14 g
Dietary Fiber: 21 g
Protein: 38 g

Mediterranean Roast Turkey Breast

This Mediterranean-inspired dish is flavorful and aromatic.

Servings: 8

- **1 boneless turkey breast (about 3 1/2-4 pounds)**
- **1 cup chicken broth, low-sodium**
- **2 tablespoons lemon juice**
- **2 medium yellow onions, chopped**
- **1/2 cup kalamata olives, pitted**
- **1 teaspoon garlic powder**
- **1 teaspoon basil**
- **1 teaspoon oregano**
- **1/2 teaspoon cinnamon**
- **1/2 teaspoon rosemary**
- **1/2 teaspoon freshly ground black pepper**
- **1 (12 ounce) jar artichoke hearts**
- **1/2 cup sun-dried tomatoes, oil-packed, sliced**

Directions:

1. Place turkey breast in slow cooker. Add chicken broth, lemon juice, onions, olives, and spices. Stir, cover, and cook on low for 6 hours.
2. Add in artichoke hearts and sun-dried tomatoes. Stir, recover, and cook an additional 30 minutes to an hour.
3. Serve over brown rice.

Nutritional information (per serving)
Calories: 356
Total Fat: 4.8 g
Sodium: 365 mg
Total Carbs: 9 g
Dietary Fiber: 1.6 g
Protein: 60 g

Jambalaya

This is a spicy Cajun dish that we've reformulated to cut the sodium way down without compromising the flavor.

Servings: 6

Ingredients:

- **1 pound chicken breast, skinless and boneless, cut into 1-2 inch chunks**
- **1/2 pound andouille sausage, crumbled**
- **2 (15 ounce) cans chopped tomatoes, no salt added**
- **1 large green bell pepper, chopped**
- **1 medium yellow onion, chopped**
- **1 cup chicken broth, low-sodium**
- **1/2 cup white wine**
- **2 teaspoons oregano**
- **1 tablespoon fresh parsley**
- **2 teaspoons Cajun seasoning**
- **1 teaspoon cayenne pepper**
- **1/2 pound medium shrimp, peeled**
- **2 cups cooked brown rice**

Directions:

1. Place all ingredients through cayenne pepper in slow cooker. Stir, cover and cook on low for 6-8 hours or on high for 3-4 hours.
2. Add in shrimp and rice. Cover and cook for an additional 30 minutes.

Nutritional information (per serving)
Calories: 430
Total Fat: 18 g
Sodium: 188 mg
Total Carbs: 23 g
Dietary Fiber: 2 g
Protein: 40 g

Honey-Glazed Chicken Wings

These wings are spicy and sweet.

Servings: 8

Ingredients:

- **1/2 cup rice wine vinegar**
- **5 tablespoons honey**
- **3 tablespoons soy sauce, low-sodium**
- **1/4 cup sesame oil**
- **2 tablespoons lemon juice**
- **3 tablespoons Asian chili paste**
- **5 cloves garlic, minced**
- **1 tablespoon freshly grated ginger (or 1/2 teaspoon dried ginger)**
- **Freshly ground black pepper, to taste**
- **2 pounds chicken wings**
- **2 tablespoons toasted sesame seeds**

Directions:

1. In a bowl, whisk together all ingredients except for chicken wings and sesame seeds.
2. Place chicken wings in slow cooker. Pour sauce over wings and stir to coat chicken.
3. Cover and cook on low for 4-5 hours or high for 2-3 hours, until chicken is cooked through.
4. Serve sprinkled with toasted sesame seeds.

Nutritional information (per serving)
Calories: 321
Total Fat: 19 g
Sodium: 428 mg
Total Carbs: 14 g
Protein: 22 g

Slow-Cooker Turkey Stroganoff

Servings: 6

Ingredients:

- 4 cups mushrooms, sliced (can use a mix of types)
- 3 medium carrots, sliced
- 1 small onion, diced
- One 3-4 pound split turkey breast, skin removed (can substitute with chicken breast)
- 1/3 cup all-purpose flour
- 1 cup nonfat Greek-style plain yogurt
- 1 tablespoon lemon juice
- 1/4 cup dry sherry (not cooking sherry)
- 1 cup frozen peas, thawed
- Freshly ground black pepper, to taste
- 12 ounces whole-wheat egg noodles, cooked
- 1/4 cup flat-leaf parsley, chopped

Directions:

1. Place mushrooms, carrots, onion, and turkey into slow cooker. Cover and cook on low for 8 hours or on high for 4 hours.
2. Remove turkey from slow cooker and cut meat from bone. Cut into bite size pieces and put back in slow cooker.
3. In a bowl, whisk together flour, yogurt, lemon juice, and sherry. Add to slow cooker along with peas and pepper. Stir, cover, and cook on high for another 20 minutes.
4. Serve over egg noodles and top with chopped parsley.

Nutritional Information (per serving)
Calories: 440
Sodium: 480 mg
Protein: 46 g
Carbs: 43 g
Fat: 6 g

Provencal Chicken and White Beans

Another very easy recipe that tastes like you spent a lot of time in the kitchen.

Servings: 6

Ingredients:

- **1 1/2 pounds chicken breast, boneless and skinless**
- **1 red bell pepper, diced**
- **1 (16 ounce) can cannellini beans, low sodium, rinsed and drained**
- **1 (14.5 ounce) can diced tomatoes, no salt added**
- **1/4 teaspoon salt**
- **1/2 teaspoon freshly ground black pepper**
- **2 teaspoons basil**
- **2 teaspoons oregano**
- **1 teaspoon thyme**

Directions:

1. Place all ingredients in slow cooker. Stir, cover, and cook on low for 7-8 hours.

Nutritional Information (per serving)
Calories: 225
Sodium: 489 mg
Protein: 29 g
Carbs: 20 g
Fat:3 g

White Chicken Chili

Servings: 6

Ingredients:

- **2 (15 ounce) cans white beans (Great Northern or cannellini), no-salt added**
- **1 pound chicken, boneless and skinless, cut into chunks**
- **1 (15 ounce) can diced tomatoes, no salt added**
- **1 (4.5 ounce) can green chilies, drained and chopped**
- **1 medium yellow onion, chopped**
- **3 cloves garlic, minced**
- **1 tablespoon chili powder**
- **1 teaspoon cumin**
- **1 teaspoon oregano**
- **1 teaspoon cayenne pepper**

Directions:

1. Add all ingredients to slow cooker. Stir to combine, cover and cook on low for 8 hours or high for 4 hours.

Nutritional Information (per serving)
Calories: 285
Sodium: 260 mg
Protein: 25 g
Carbs: 34 g
Dietary Fiber: 8 g
Fat: 5.7 g

Meat Dishes

(Beef, Pork, Lamb, Veal)

Barbecued Pork

Servings: 6-8

Ingredients:

- **½ pound pork cutlets, boneless**
- **1 cup celery, chopped**
- **1 medium onion, chopped**
- **2 cloves garlic, minced**
- **1 teaspoon olive oil**
- **1 6-ounce can tomato paste, no salt added**
- **1 8-ounce can tomato sauce, no salt added**
- **2 tablespoons white vinegar**
- **1 teaspoon Worcestershire sauce**
- **2 teaspoons chopped parsley**
- **1/4 teaspoon pepper**
- **1/2 teaspoon garlic powder**
- **1 tablespoon packed brown sugar**
- **1 teaspoon chili powder**

Directions:

1. Cut pork cutlets into 1-2 inch cubes.
2. Heat olive oil in large skillet over medium heat. Add pork cubes and brown on all sides, about 4-5 minutes. Place in slow cooker. Add celery, onion, and garlic to skillet and sauté until they begin to soften, 2-3 minutes. Add to slow cooker with pork.
3. In a bowl, combine sauce ingredients (tomato paste through chili powder), and then pour into slow cooker over pork and vegetables. Stir to combine.
4. Cover and cook on low for 7-8 hours or high for 5-6 hours.

Nutritional Information (per serving)
Calories: 335.0
Total Fat: 13.5 g
Sodium: 115.0 mg
Total Carbs: 9.9 g
Dietary Fiber: 1.4 g
Protein: 42.7 g

Slow Cooker Chili

Servings: 11 (1 cup servings)

Ingredients:

- **1 cup dry pinto beans**
- **1 cup dry dark red kidney beans**
- **1 cup light red kidney beans**
- **1 cup water**
- **½ pound ground turkey**
- **½ pound lean ground beef**
- **3 medium yellow onions, chopped**
- **1 large green bell pepper, chopped**
- **1 large red bell pepper, chopped**
- **3 cloves garlic, minced**
- **6 large tomatoes, chopped**
- **1 teaspoon cayenne pepper**
- **1 tablespoon cumin**
- **1/2 tablespoon marjoram**
- **1 teaspoon freshly ground black pepper**
- **1 tablespoon chili powder**
- **1 tablespoon oregano**

Directions:

1. Place beans in large bowl, cover with water, and soak overnight. Rinse and drain well.
2. Heat a large skillet over medium heat. Add ground beef and ground turkey and cook until browned. Add browned meat to slow cooker. In same pan, sauté onions, pepper, and garlic until just softened, about 3-4 minutes. Add to slow cooker.

67

3. Add soaked and drained beans, chopped tomatoes, and spices to slow cooker. Stir well.
4. Cover and cook for 7-8 hours on low.

Nutritional Information (per serving)

Calories: 181.8

Total Fat: 3.5 g

Sodium: 63.0 mg

Total Carbs: 33.0 g

Dietary Fiber: 15.0 g

Protein: 18.4 g

Spaghetti Sauce with Meat and Vegetables

Jarred sauce typically has a large amount of sodium. Make your own and sneak in some extra veggies too.

Servings: 6-8

Ingredients:

- ½ pound ground turkey
- ½ pound ground beef, lean
- 1 large yellow onion, diced fine
- 3 cloves garlic, minced
- 1 green pepper, diced fine
- 1 medium zucchini, diced
- 1 medium yellow/crookneck squash, diced
- 1 pound sliced mushrooms
- 1 6-ounce can tomato paste, no salt added
- 6 large tomatoes, diced
- 1 cup red wine
- 1 tablespoon garlic powder
- 1 tablespoon oregano
- 1/2 tablespoon dried basil
- 1 tablespoon Italian seasoning
- Freshly ground black pepper, to taste

Directions:

1. Heat large nonstick skillet over medium heat. Add ground turkey and beef and cook until browned. Add browned meat to slow cooker.
2. In the same skillet used to cook the ground meat heat onion, bell pepper, zucchini, squash, mushrooms, and garlic until just softened, about 3-4 minutes. Add to slow cooker along with the meat.
3. Add tomato paste, chopped tomatoes, wine, and spices, stir well.
4. Cover and cook on low 6-7 hours.

Nutritional Information (per serving)

Calories: 291.1

Total Fat: 6.4 g

Sodium: 91.3 mg

Total Carbs: 28.0 g

Dietary Fiber: 7.2 g

Protein: 21.4 g

Slow Cooker Bolognese Sauce

This sauce has a distinct, rich, meaty flavor.

Servings: 8

Ingredients:

- 4 slices bacon, cut into small pieces
- 1 tablespoon olive oil
- 1 medium yellow onion, diced
- 1 carrot, chopped fine
- 2 celery stalks, chopped fine
- 1 pound ground beef, lean
- ½ cup tomato paste, no salt added
- ½ cup milk, reduced fat
- 1 ½ cups beef stock, low sodium
- ½ cup red wine
- 1 teaspoon dried basil
- 1 teaspoon dried oregano
- Freshly ground black pepper, to taste

Directions:

1. Sauté bacon in large frying pan for 5 minutes over medium heat. Add olive oil, onion, carrots, and celery and cook for another 5-6 minutes. Add ground beef to pan and cook until browned, stirring occasionally, about 4-5 minutes.
2. Add tomato paste, milk, beef stock, and red wine to slow cooker. Stir well to dissolve tomato paste. Add meat mixture to slow cooker. Season with salt and pepper.
3. Cover and cook on low for 6 hours.

Nutritional Information (per serving)
Calories: 175
Total Fat: 9 g
Sodium: 157 mg
Total Carbs: 7 g
Protein: 15 g

Mexican Beef Stew

This hearty stew is a flavorful twist on traditional beef stew.

Servings: 6

Ingredients:

- 1 pound beef stew meat, cut into 1-inch cubes
- 2 tablespoons all-purpose flour
- 1 tablespoon olive oil
- 1 (15 ounce) can black beans, no salt-added, rinsed and drained
- 2 medium carrots, sliced
- 1 medium onion, chopped
- 2 cloves garlic, minced
- 1 (14.5 ounce) can diced tomatoes, no salt added
- 1 (14.5 ounce) can low-sodium beef broth
- 2 teaspoons chili powder
- 1 teaspoon ground cumin
- 1/2 teaspoon freshly ground black pepper
- 1/2 teaspoon crushed red pepper
- 1 cup frozen corn kernels
- 1 avocado, peeled, pitted, and cubed (optional)

Directions:

1. Place beef cubes in a bowl, sprinkle with flour. Stir to coat beef with flour.
2. Heat olive oil in a skillet over medium-high heat. Add beef cubes and brown beef on all sides, about 5 minutes.
3. Add beef, beans, carrots, onion, garlic, diced tomatoes, beef broth, and spices to slow cooker. Stir to combine.
4. Cover and cook on low for 7 hours or until beef is tender.
5. Add corn kernels and stir gently. Recover and cook for another 15 minutes.
6. Serve topped with avocado cubes.

Nutritional information (per serving)
Calories: 272
Total Fat: 9 g
Sodium: 456 mg
Total Carbs: 27 g
Protein: 22 g

Lamb Tagine with Pears

Tagines are slow-cooked meats, vegetables, and fruits that easily adapted to a slow cooker.

Servings: 5
Ingredients:

- 1 tablespoon olive oil
- 2 medium onions, sliced
- 2 pounds lamb meat, cut into 1 to 2 inch cubes
- 2 teaspoons cumin
- 2 teaspoons coriander
- 1 teaspoon ginger
- 1 teaspoon cinnamon
- 1 teaspoon freshly ground black pepper, to taste

- 1 1/2 cups chicken broth, low-sodium
- 1 bay leaf
- 1 tablespoon lemon juice
- 4 pears, peeled, cored, and cut into 1 inch cubes
- 1/2 cup golden raisins
- 1/2 cup slivered almonds, blanched

Directions:

1. Heat olive oil in large skillet over medium heat, add onions and sauté for 2-3 minutes. Add in lamb meat and continue to cook, stirring, until lamb is browned on all sides. Add lamb and onions to slow cooker.
2. Season with cumin, coriander, ginger, cinnamon, and black pepper. Pour in chicken broth, and add in bay leaf and lemon juice. Cover and cook on low for 6-7 hours or high for 4-5 hours or until meat is tender.
3. Add in pears, raisins, and almonds, recover and cook on low for another 15 minutes or until pears are soft.
4. Serve over couscous.

Nutritional information (per serving)
Calories: 394
Total Fat: 14.5 g
Sodium: 246 mg
Total Carbs: 42 g
Dietary Fiber: 7.5 g
Protein: 26.5 g

Moroccan Beef Tagine

Cooking this dish in the slow cooker allows the flavors to deepen and develop.

Servings: 4 to 6
Ingredients:
Spice rub

- **1 tablespoon cumin**
- **1 tablespoon cinnamon**
- **1 tablespoon ginger**
- **1 tablespoon paprika**
- **1 teaspoon nutmeg**
- **1 teaspoon turmeric**
- **1/2 teaspoon sea salt**
- **1 teaspoon freshly ground black pepper**

For the stew

- **1 ½ pounds stew beef**
- **2 tablespoon olive oil**
- **1 medium onion, chopped**
- **1 bunch fresh coriander**
- **1 (14 ounce) can chopped tomatoes**
- **3 cups vegetable or beef stock, low-sodium**
- **1 small zucchini, chopped**
- **1 large carrot, sliced thin**
- **1 red bell pepper, sliced thin**
- **3-4 prunes, chopped**
- **Freshly ground black pepper, to taste**

Directions:

1. In a small bowl mix together all of the ingredients for the spice rub.
2. Place beef in large zip lock bag. Add spice mixture and shake to thoroughly coat meat. Put in refrigerator for a couple of hours or overnight.

3. Heat olive oil in large skillet over medium heat. Add beef and brown on all sides, about 5 minutes.
4. Add meat to slow cooker. Add all remaining ingredients. Stir to combine.
5. Cover and cook on high setting for 5-6 hours or low setting for 7-8 hours.

Nutritional information (per serving)
Calories: 338
Total Fat: 17 g
Sodium: 329 mg
Total Carbs: 18 g
Protein: 26 g

Slow-Cooker Beef Stew Provencal

Servings: 10

Ingredients:

Bouquet garni

- **Cheesecloth**
- **1 bay leaf**
- **1 stalk celery, chopped**
- **3 sprigs fresh parsley**
- **3 sprigs fresh thyme**

Stew

- **2 tablespoons extra-virgin olive oil, divided**
- **3 pounds beef chuck (or other stew meat), cut into 1-inch pieces**
- **3 teaspoons kosher salt, divided**
- **1/2 teaspoon freshly ground pepper, divided**
- **3 medium yellow onions, chopped**
- **4 cloves garlic, minced**
- **3-4 large carrots, sliced into 1-inch rounds**
- **3 tablespoons tomato paste, no salt added**
- **1 pound mushrooms, sliced**
- **1 quart beef stock, low-sodium**
- **1/4 cup red wine**

Directions:

1. To assemble bouquet garni, cut a square of cheesecloth. Place bay leaf, celery, parsley, and thyme in center. Tie with kitchen twine.

2. To prepare stew heat 1 tablespoon olive oil in large heavy-duty pan. Add beef cubes and cook until browned on all sides. Transfer to slow cooker, season with 1 teaspoon salt and black pepper.
3. Add another tablespoon of oil to pan and add onions, garlic, and carrots. Cook, stirring occasionally until they begin to soften, about 4-5 minutes. Season with remaining salt and pepper. Add to slow cooker with beef.
4. Add tomato paste, mushrooms, beef stock, red wine, and bouquet garni to slow cooker. Stir to combine.
5. Cover and cook on low setting for 8-9 hours or high setting for 5-6 hours.

Nutritional Information (per serving)

Calories: 351

Sodium: 380 mg

Protein: 26 g

Carbs: 14 g

Dietary Fiber: 5 g

Fat: 15 g

Slow-Cooked Beef Roast

Servings: 8

Ingredients:

- 1 tablespoon olive oil
- 1 chuck beef roast (3 pounds)
- 1/2 teaspoon salt
- 1 teaspoon black pepper
- 2 cups low-sodium beef broth
- 6 large carrots, sliced
- 3 medium onions, diced
- 2 cups mushrooms, sliced
- 3 cloves garlic, minced
- 3 stalks celery, diced
- 2 tablespoons tomato paste
- 1 tablespoon Worcestershire sauce
- 2 sprigs fresh thyme
- tablespoons all-purpose flour

Directions:

1. Heat oil in a large skillet over medium-high heat. Sprinkle roast with salt and pepper. Place roast in pan and brown on all sides, about 5 minutes. Put roast in slow cooker.
2. Add remaining ingredients except for flour. Stir, cover, and cook on low for 7-8 hours or high for 3-4 hours, until roast is cooked through.
3. Remove a 1/4 cup of broth from slow cooker and place in small bowl. Add flow and mix until flour is dissolved. Add back into slow cooker and stir. Remove and discard thyme sprigs.
4. Slice roast and top with vegetables and sauce.

Nutritional Information (per serving)
Calories: 284
Sodium: 424 mg
Protein: 31 g
Carbs: 17 g
Dietary Fiber: 1.5 g
Fat: 9 g

Beef Stew with Butternut Squash

This aromatic stew with just a hint of sweetness is perfect for a crisp autumn day.

Servings: 4

Ingredients:

- **3 tablespoons olive oil**
- **1 medium yellow onion, diced**
- **3 cloves garlic, minced**
- **2 pounds stew beef, cut into cubes**
- **1 can (16 ounces) diced tomatoes, no salt added**
- **1 large butternut squash, trimmed and cut into bite-size cubes**
- **4 cups beef broth, low-sodium**
- **1 tablespoon rosemary**
- **1 tablespoon thyme**
- **Freshly ground black pepper, to taste**

Directions:

1. Heat olive oil in large pot over medium heat. Add onions and garlic and sauté for 2-3 minutes. Add the beef cubes and cook until the beef is browned, about 5 minutes.
2. Transfer to slow cooker. Add the diced tomatoes, butternut squash, beef broth, rosemary, and thyme. Set cooker to low setting and cook for 8 hours. Add salt and freshly ground black pepper to taste.

Nutritional Information (per serving)
Calories: 580
Sodium: 292 mg
Protein: 51 g
Carbs: 8 g
Fat: 36 g

Irish Stew

This is a hearty stew.

Servings: 6-8

Ingredients:

- **2 pounds lamb roast, cut into 1" pieces**
- **1lb small red potatoes, cut into bite size pieces**
- **1 medium onion, sliced**
- **2 large carrots, sliced**
- **1 large parsnip, sliced**
- **3 stalks celery, chopped**
- **3 cups chicken broth, low sodium**
- **2 teaspoon fresh thyme, chopped**
- **1/2 teaspoon sea salt**
- **1 teaspoon pepper**

Directions:

1. Combine all ingredients in slow cooker. Stir to combine.
2. Cover and cook on low for 8 hours.

Nutritional Information (per serving)

Calories: 269

Sodium: 257 mg

Protein: 39 g

Carbs: 20 g

Fat: 7 g

Cider Pork Roast

This is a very tender and flavorful pork roast.

Servings: 8
Ingredients:

- 1 teaspoon ground ginger
- 1/4 teaspoon salt
- 1/2 teaspoon freshly ground black pepper
- 3 tablespoons all-purpose flour
- 1 pork loin roast (3 pounds)
- 1 tablespoon olive oil
- 1 medium yellow onion, chopped
- 1 apple, peeled, cored, and chopped
- 3 cloves garlic, minced
- 2 stalks celery, chopped
- 4 carrots, sliced
- 2 cups apple cider
- 1 1/2 cups water

Directions:

1. Combine ginger, salt, pepper, and flour in a bowl. Sprinkle flour mixture over roast, covering all sides.
2. In a large skillet, heat oil over medium-high heat. Add roast and brown on all sides, about 5 minutes.
3. Place roast in slow cooker. Add all remaining ingredients. Cover and cook on low for 6-7 hours or on high for 3-4 hours, until pork is cooked through.

Nutritional Information (per serving)
Calories: 235
Sodium: 125 mg
Protein: 21 g
Carbs: 20 g
Dietary Fiber: 2 g
Fat: 8 g

Vegetable Dishes

Baked Potatoes with Broccoli and Mushrooms

You may not think about baking potatoes in a slow cooker but it is an easy way to make them and they come out moist and delicious. These veggie-topped potatoes make a meal in themselves.

Servings: 4

Ingredients:

- 4 medium baking potatoes, washed
- 2 tablespoons olive oil, divided
- 1/2 pound mushrooms, sliced
- 1 bunch broccoli, cut into small florets
- 1/3 cup broth (vegetable, chicken, or beef), hot, low-sodium
- Freshly ground black pepper, to taste
- 2/3 cup plain yogurt, low-fat

Directions:

1. Make sure potatoes are completely dry. Rub potatoes with 1 tablespoon of olive oil. Wrap each potato in aluminum foil. Place in slow cooker, cover, and cook on low setting for 7-8 hours or high setting for 4-5 hours, until potatoes are tender.
2. Heat remaining tablespoon of olive oil in a large skillet over medium heat. Add mushrooms and broccoli and sauté until broccoli is tender but not soft, about 10 minutes.
3. Unwrap each potato from foil. Make slice in center of potatoes and scoop out potato into bowl. Add broth, pepper, and yogurt. Mix to combine. Divide mixture and stuff back into potato skins. Top with broccoli and mushrooms.

Nutritional information (per serving)
Calories: 330
Total Fat: 7 g
Sodium: 360 mg
Total Carbs: 57 g
Dietary Fiber: 8 g
Protein: 14 g

Mediterranean Vegetable Stew

This is a really easy stew that makes a nice, light vegetarian meal. Serve over brown rice or orzo.

Servings: 10

Ingredients:

- 1 butternut squash, peeled and cubed
- 1 eggplant, cubed
- 1 large zucchini, cubed
- 1 medium yellow onion, chopped
- 1 tomato, diced
- 1 carrot, sliced thin
- 2 cloves garlic, minced
- 1 cup tomato sauce, low-sodium (homemade or store bought)
- 1/2 cup vegetable broth, low-sodium
- 1/2 teaspoon ground cumin
- 1/2 teaspoon turmeric
- 1/2 teaspoon crushed red pepper
- 1/4 teaspoon cinnamon
- 1/4 teaspoon paprika

Directions:

1. Combine all ingredients in slow cooker. Stir, cover, and cook on low for 7-8 hours or high for 4-5 hours, or until vegetables are tender.

Nutritional information (per serving)
Calories: 122
Total Fat: .5 g
Sodium: 157 mg
Total Carbs: 30 g
Dietary Fiber: 7.8 g
Protein: 3.4 g

Sweet Potato Coconut Curry

This is a mild curry that makes a delicious side to fish or chicken.
Servings: 4
Ingredients:

- **1 tablespoon olive oil**
- **1 small yellow onion, diced**
- **3 clove garlic, minced**
- **1 teaspoon cumin powder**
- **½ teaspoon turmeric**
- **½ teaspoon cardamom**
- **½ teaspoon cinnamon**
- **½ teaspoon ground ginger**
- **1 (14.5 ounce) can diced tomatoes, no salt added**
- **4 medium sweet potatoes, peeled and cut into bit-size cubes**
- **1 can (14 ounces) coconut milk**
- **Freshly ground black pepper, to taste**
- **Flat leaf parsley for garnish**

Directions:

1. Add all ingredients to slow cooker. Mix to combine.
2. Cover and cook on low setting for 4-5 hours until sweet potatoes are tender.
3. Serve hot, topped with fresh parsley for garnish.

Nutritional information (per serving)
Calories: 174
Total Fat: 10 g
Sodium: 36 mg
Total Carbs: 20 g
Protein: 4 g

Slow Cooker Baked Beans

These beans take a while but have a taste you just can't get from canned baked beans.

Servings: 8

Ingredients:

- **1 pound dry great Northern beans**
- **8 cups water**
- **4 ounces salt pork, diced**
- **1 medium yellow onion, chopped**
- **1/2 cup molasses**
- **1/3 cup brown sugar, packed**
- **1 teaspoon dry mustard**
- **2 tablespoons cider vinegar**
- **1/2 teaspoon freshly ground black pepper**

Directions:

1. In a large saucepan, bring beans and water to a boil. Cook for 2 hours. Place pan with beans and water, covered, into refrigerator overnight.
2. The next day, pour beans and 1 1/2 cups of their liquid into slow cooker. Add in salt pork, molasses, brown sugar, dry mustard, and black pepper. Cover and cook on low for 12-14 hours.

Nutritional information (per serving)
Calories: 365
Total Fat: 12 g
Sodium: 215 mg
Total Carbs: 54 g
Dietary Fiber: 1.7 g
Protein: 12 g

Moroccan Root Vegetable Tagine

Subtly spiced, this vegetarian dish makes a nice meal served with couscous.

Servings: 8

Ingredients:

- **1 pound parsnips, peeled and cubed**
- **1 pound sweet potatoes, peeled and cubed**
- **2 medium yellow onions, chopped**
- **1 pound carrots, chopped**
- **12 dried apricots, chopped**
- **8 prunes, pitted and chopped**
- **2 teaspoons turmeric**
- **2 teaspoons cumin**
- **1 teaspoon ground ginger**
- **1 teaspoon cinnamon**
- **1/2 teaspoon cayenne pepper**
- **1 tablespoon dried parsley**
- **1 tablespoon cilantro**
- **3 cups vegetable broth, low-sodium**

Directions:

1. Place vegetables in slow cooker. Season with spices and stir to coat. Pour in vegetable broth.
2. Cover and cook for 5-6 hours on low or 3-4 hours on high, or until vegetables are tender.
3. Serve with couscous.

Nutritional information (per serving)
Calories: 171
Total Fat: .7 g
Sodium: 188 mg
Total Carbs: 38 g
Dietary Fiber: 8.7 g
Protein: 3.4 g

Vegetarian Vegetable Stew

This is perfect as a side dish or a light meal.

Servings: 6

Ingredients:

- **4 large carrots, sliced**
- **2 medium turnips, peeled and cubes**
- **1 large onion, sliced thin**
- **3 garlic cloves, minced**
- **1 zucchini, sliced**
- **2 yellow squash, sliced**
- **2 cups vegetable broth, low-sodium**
- **1/2 teaspoon red pepper flakes**
- **1 teaspoon thyme**
- **Freshly ground black pepper, to taste**

Directions:

1. Combine all ingredients in slow cooker.
2. Cover, and cook on low for 5-6 hours or on high for 3-4 hours.

Nutritional information (per serving)
Calories: 55
Total Fat: 0 g
Sodium: 112 mg
Total Carbs: 13 g
Protein: 2 g

Desserts

Slow Cooker Brown Rice Pudding

Servings: 6

Ingredients:

- **2/3 cup brown rice, long grain**
- **1 teaspoon cinnamon**
- **1/4 cup honey**
- **1 2/3 cups milk, low-fat**
- **1 (13.5 ounce can) coconut milk, low-fat**
- **1 teaspoon vanilla extract**
- **1/2 cup raisins (optional)**

Directions:

1. Add all ingredients through coconut milk to slow cooker. Stir to combine. Cover and cook on low for 3-4 hours until desired consistency is reached.
2. Add vanilla and raisins, stir, recover slow cooker and turn off. Let sit for 15 minutes before serving.

Nutritional information (per serving)
Calories: 245
Total Fat: 14 g
Sodium: 50 mg
Total Carbs: 29 g
Dietary Fiber: 1 g
Protein: 4 g

Berry Cobbler

Servings: 8
Ingredients:

- **1 1/4 cups all-purpose flour, divided**
- **1 cup sugar plus 2 tablespoons, divided**
- **1 teaspoon baking powder**
- **1/2 teaspoon cinnamon**
- **1 egg, beaten**
- **1/4 cup skim milk**
- **2 tablespoons olive oil**
- **1/8 teaspoon salt**
- **2 cups raspberries, fresh or frozen (thawed)**
- **2 cups blueberries, fresh or frozen (thawed)**
- **Vanilla yogurt for topping (optional)**

Directions:

1. Combine 1 cup flour, 2 tablespoon sugar, baking powder and cinnamon in a large bowl.
2. In a separate bowl, mix together the egg, milk, and oil. Fold in dry ingredients until just moistened (batter will be thick).
3. Spray bottom of slow cooker with nonstick spray. Spread batter evenly into bottom of slow cooker.
4. In a large bowl, combine the salt and remaining flour and sugar; add berries and toss to coat. Spread over batter.
5. Cover and cook on high for 2 to 2-1/2 hours or until a toothpick inserted into cobbler comes out clean.
6. Serve topped with yogurt.

Nutritional information (per serving)
Calories: 250
Total Fat: 4 g
Sodium: 140 mg
Total Carbs: 51 g
Dietary Fiber: 4 g
Protein: 3 g

Apple Crisp

Really delicious and super easy in the slow cooker.

Servings: 6

Ingredients:

- 1 cup all-purpose flour
- 1/2 cup oats
- 1/2 cup brown sugar, packed
- 2/3 cup white sugar, divided
- 1 1/2 teaspoons cinnamon, divided
- 1/2 teaspoon nutmeg
- Pinch of salt
- 4 tablespoons butter, cut into pieces
- 1 cup walnuts, chopped
- 1 tablespoon cornstarch
- 1 teaspoon ginger
- 6 cups apples (about 6-7 large apples), peeled, cored, and cubed
- 2 tablespoons lemon juice

Directions:

1. In a bowl, mix together flour, oats, brown sugar, 1/3 cup white sugar, 1 teaspoon cinnamon, nutmeg, and salt. Add in butter pieces and use hands or fork to mix together until crumbs form. Stir in walnuts.
2. In a separate bowl, mix together 1/3 cup sugar, cornstarch, ginger, and 1/2 teaspoon cinnamon.
3. Place apples in slow cooker. Stir in sugar and cornstarch mixture. Sprinkle on lemon juice and stir. Sprinkle butter and walnut mixture evenly on top. Cover and cook on low for 3-4 hours or high for 2 hours or until apples are tender.

Nutritional information (per serving)
Calories: 565
Total Fat: 29 g
Sodium: 118 mg
Total Carbs: 84 g
Dietary Fiber: 6 g
Protein: 6 g

Spiced Applesauce

This applesauce is easy and makes a nice, warm, healthy treat on a cold day.

Servings: 8

Ingredients:

- **8 apples, peeled, cored, and sliced (can use a combination, Granny Smith, Gala, Golden Delicious, etc.)**
- **1/3 cup water**
- **1/3 cup brown sugar, packed**
- **1/2 teaspoon pumpkin pie spice**
- **1/4 teaspoon nutmeg**

Directions:

1. Combine all ingredients in slow cooker. Stir, cover and cook on low for 6 to 8 hours.

Nutritional information (per serving)

Calories: 98

Total Fat: .2 g

Sodium: 3 mg

Total Carbs: 26 g

Dietary Fiber: 1.7 g

Protein: .4 g

From the Author

I hope you enjoyed the *DASH Diet Slow Cooker Recipes: Easy, Delicious, and Healthy Recipes* and that it helps you create easy, healthy DASH Diet meals for you and your family to enjoy!

Please check out our other titles in the DASH Diet series:

DASH Diet for Weight Loss

DASH Diet for Beginners

DASH Diet Cookbook: Quick and Easy DASH Diet Recipes

Mason Jar Meals by Dylanna Press

Mason jar meals are a fun and practical way to take your meals on the go. Mason jars are an easy way to prepare individual servings, so whether you're cooking for one, two, or a whole crowd, these fun, make-ahead meals will work.

Includes More than 50 Recipes and Full-Color Photos

In this book, you'll find a wide variety of recipes including all kinds of salads, as well as hot meal ideas such as mini chicken pot pies and lasagna in a jar. Also included are mouth-watering desserts such as strawberry shortcake, apple pie, and s'mores.

The recipes are easy to prepare and don't require any special cooking skills. So what are you waiting for? Grab your Mason jars and start preparing these gorgeous and tasty dishes!

The Inflammation Diet by Dylanna Press

Beat Pain, Slow Aging, and Reduce Risk of Heart Disease with the Inflammation Diet

Inflammation has been called the "silent killer" and it has been linked to a wide variety of illnesses including heart disease, arthritis, diabetes, chronic pain, autoimmune disorders, and cancer.

Often, the root of chronic inflammation is in the foods we eat.

The Inflammation Diet: Complete Guide to Beating Pain and Inflammation will show you how, by making simple changes to your diet, you can greatly reduce inflammation in your body and reduce your symptoms and lower your risk of chronic disease.

The book includes a complete plan for eliminating inflammation and implementing an anti-inflammatory diet:

• Overview of inflammation and the body's immune response – what can trigger it and why chronic inflammation is harmful
• The link between diet and inflammation
• Inflammatory foods to avoid
• Anti-inflammatory foods to add to your diet to beat pain and inflammation
• Over 50 delicious inflammation diet recipes
• A 14-day meal plan

Take charge of your health and implement the inflammation diet to lose weight, slow the aging process, eliminate chronic pain, and reduce the likelihood and symptoms of chronic disease.

Learn how to heal your body from within through diet.

Index

Made in the USA
Lexington, KY
21 April 2016